THE
Old Photographs
SERIES

AROUND
BRIDPORT

Four generations of the Hussey family, three of which have been in baking in Bridport since 1911 when George Hussey (right) began the family business at 91 East Street. George's father Harry is seated in front, his oldest son Len, with daughter Ann, is on his right. The business moved to West Street (see p.48) in 1922 where, under Michael, the fourth generation of baking Husseys, the business continues to enjoy its reputation as first-class bakers.

THE
Old Photographs
SERIES

AROUND BRIDPORT

Compiled by
Les Berry and Gerald Gosling

**ALAN
SUTTON**

BATH • AUGUSTA • RENNES

First published 1994
Copyright © Les Berry and Gerald Gosling 1994

Alan Sutton Limited
12 Riverside Court
Bath BA2 3DZ

ISBN 07524 0006 1

Typesetting and origination by
Alan Sutton Limited
Printed in Great Britain

Contents

The history of Bridport has, literally, been tied up with rope and net making; and the expressions a 'Bridport Dagger' or a 'Bridport Necktie' were the 18th-century criminal's slang for that particular piece of the town's produce that might await him at Tyburn. Twentieth-century Bridport sees the town's products ending up in more peaceful directions such as football nets, seen here being made at Edwards's in 1959 by the Croad brothers, Bill (left) and Ron. Local nets have graced many an international and FA Cup Final.

Introduction

To introduce a book about Bridport is a very special honour, for Bridport is a very special town. I discovered the bustling market town back in 1977 as a visiting grockle, who returned at least once a year thereafter to recharge her batteries in what seemed to be a spiritual home.

And so when the time came and my family had grown, I know where I wanted to be, and finally arrived here in mid-1988. Such a short time ago and yet I now know more people, more places, more history than in any other place I have lived. This good fortune can be attributed to two things: the friendliness of the inhabitants and my job.

I was lucky enough to land a position with the *Bridport News* in East Street, immediately after moving, since when the work has been an ever-growing source of interest and local contact. One and a half centuries is but a blink in the evolution of our planet, yet it seems an awfully long time when one recalls that the history of Bridport has been faithfully chronicled by the *Bridport News* since 23 June 1855.

It is a truly lovely place to write in and about, but such a successful town had to have an industrial basis on which to build. Much of Bridport's workaday life was spent in the staple trade: the making of cordage, twine and nets. Bridport is said (probably with some truth) to have supplied the cordage and ropes for the ships that chased the Spanish Armada up the Channel; it has certainly supplied the Royal Navy ever since. The Poet Laureate Drayton wrote at the start of the 16th century:

> To Bert-port which hath gained
> That praise from every place, and worthilie obtain'd
> Our cordage from her store, and cables should be made,
> Of any in that kind most fit for marine trade.

But it has not been only the Royal Navy that has made use of Bridport's rope. Many a wrong-doer met his gruesome end on Tyburn Tree, where the noose became known as a 'Bridport Dagger' or a 'Bridport Necktie'.

Rope and nets are still made in the town, much of the production being used in such varied sports as deck-tennis, netball, greyhound racing, ice hockey, and, not least, for the goal nets which have not only graced many an international football match and FA Cup final, but are even said to have been 'invented' in the town. A local firm, William Edwards and Son, certainly held the patent for such nets for many years.

Bridport, however, abounds with a history rich in other directions than rope. Its oldest building is St Mary's church, built around 1350-80 on the site of an older building and containing an eight-bell peal, two of which date from 1630 and 1631. There are many other treasures in the town, not least the Chantry in South Street, which legend links with an underground passage to the church. Hard by are the Daniel Taylor Almshouses, older than their 1696 conveyance as such for the poor of the town, and the museum, once thought to be the home of a Charity Priest.

Bridport's wide main streets were once much narrower; however the pavements, as shown in some of the photographs, were wider through being used as line walks by twine makers in bygone times. The handsome buildings that line the pavements deserve better than your average shopper's window-only glance. Above Bridport's thriving commercial centre can be seen many a fine old building, not least the former George Inn that became the Beach & Company Chemists and Druggists in 1788, and is where Charles II is said to have called in during his wanderings around Bridport and Charmouth after the ill-fated Battle of Worcester (1651), when he was looking for a vessel to take him to France. Out on the Dorchester Road the King Charles Stone marks the spot where he fled up a side lane.

The town is the centre of some lovely countryside and villages which show Dorset at its very best. Charmouth, Chideock, Golden Cap and the Char Valley to the west; Beaminster and Netherbury to the north; West Bay (Bridport Harbour) and Burton Bradstock to the south and east.

Sadly, present-day Bridport has not escaped the recession. It is a continuing grief to watch old, established businesses closing; and to see lovely, mature buildings boarded up. How delightful then, to turn the pages of this book and find the town as it once was – and surely will be again. Its spirited prosperity has been faithfully chronicled by Les Berry and Gerald Gosling, who indeed have done the whole neighbourhood proud with this pictorial history. It deserves every success.

Rosemary Lewis

One
Bridport and its Harbour
The Place

HMS *Bridport* in 1941. The coastal patrol boat was built in 1940 from the proceedings of Bridport's 'War Weapons Week'. After the war the vessel was transferred to the RAF and used for air-sea rescue purposes. Its bell is displayed in Bridport's Town Hall.

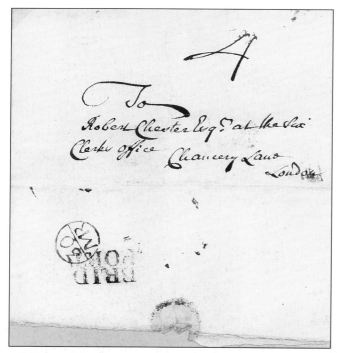

One of the earliest-known Bridport letters and sent to Robert Chester, Esq. at the Clerks Office, Chancery Lane, London, on 30 March 1767. The manuscript '4' above the address indicates that the letter would cost four pence (paid by the recipient, of course; the introduction of the famous 'Penny Black' and a universal penny post in 1840 changed all that). The postmark is the 'two-line' BRIDPORT as opposed to the 'one-line' type also in use around that time.

The Royal Mail at Bridport Post Office, 1910. The general post office in East Street, now John Menzies, was opened on 23 July 1890. Before that it occupied premises on the opposite side of the street (now the Midland Bank). Its present home in West Street is Granville House, the one-time home of Dr Ralph and Mrs Frieda Stanford. Apart from the obligatory gathering for any street picture of the time, the most interesting things here are the clothes worn by the driver and his 'mate', which are more in keeping with Oxford undergraduates than postal employees.

George Bondfield (far left) outside his garage in East Street, Bridport, 1906. George, whose father had made steam engines for Gundry's, opened these premises around 1903, but moved within a few years to the site in West Street where Howard, the fourth generation of the family, is now in charge.

North Mills Lake, Bridport, seen above around 1926, was the scene of mayorial discomfiture back in 1891, when Mr Tucker, the current mayor, led the revival of the ancient custom of beating the bounds which had been in abeyance since 1832. As the bottom picture shows, the incident reached the national press (*Daily Graphic*). The route of the beaters, and the parish boundary, led across the centre of the mill-pond; and His Worship, with the borough surveyor and a 'lad' (someone had to do the actual work), tried to cross on a specially constructed raft. Near the middle they capsized. Mr Tucker (said to be the swimmer on the left) and the lad made it to the shore; the surveyor, presumably a non-swimmer, had to be rescued. The mills once belonged to the Hounsell family, prominent in the rope and net trade in Bridport from around 1625. Hounsells eventually became Bridport Industries Ltd and amalgamated with Joseph Gundry & Co in 1963, forming the present Bridport Gundry Ltd. North Mills is now the site of an industrial estate.

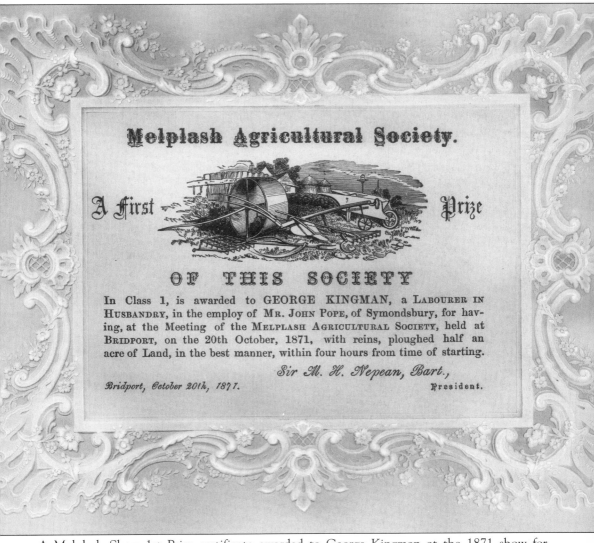

Melplash Agricultural Society.

A First ⁖ Prize

OF THIS SOCIETY

In Class 1, is awarded to GEORGE KINGMAN, a LABOURER IN HUSBANDRY, in the employ of MR. JOHN POPE, of Symondsbury, for having, at the Meeting of the MELPLASH AGRICULTURAL SOCIETY, held at BRIDPORT, on the 20th October, 1871, with reins, ploughed half an acre of Land, in the best manner, within four hours from time of starting.

Sir M. H. Nepean, Bart.,

Bridport, October 20th, 1871.

President.

A Melplash Show 1st Prize certificate awarded to George Kingman at the 1871 show for ploughing, in the 'best manner' no less! The show, now one of the West Country's leading agricultural events and held on a permanent site between Bridport and West Bay, owes its origins to a quarrel between two farm labourers from Melplash. Deep in their cups in the Half Moon one night they argued over who was the better ploughman; the resulting match became the annual event from which the show descends.

MELPLAISH
AGRICULTURAL SOCIETY.

PRESIDENT FOR 1867.

JOHN FLOYER, Esq., M.P.

VICE-PRESIDENTS :

Thos. Colfox, Esq.
William Colfox, Esq.
Joseph Gundry, Esq.
Benjamin P. Gundry, Esq.
J. P. Gundry, Esq.
Arthur Martin, Esq.

J. M. P. Montagu, Esq.
The Hon. W. H. B. Portman, M.P.
G. Sturt, Esq., M.P.
Reg. Thornton, Esq.
Charles Weld, Esq.

THE
ANNUAL MEETING

Of this Society will be held at Melplaish,

On Friday, the 18th October, 1867,

When the following Prizes will be awarded.

PRIZES FOR STOCK.

	£	s	d
For the best pair of horses for agricultural purposes, that shall have worked in the ploughing match ...	2	0	0
For the second best...	1	0	0
For the best cart colt, under three years of age ...	1	0	0
For the best hack, under three years of age	1	0	0
Each of the above to have been in the exhibitor's possession six months.			
For the best horn ram of any age	1	0	0
For the best pair of horn ram lambs, under one year of age	1	0	0
For the best twelve horn ewes, two, four, and six-tooth, four of each head	2	0	0
For the best twenty chilver horn lambs	2	0	0
For the best Down ram of any age	1	0	0
For the best pair of Down ram lambs under one year	1	0	0
For the best twelve Down ewes, two, four, and six-tooth, four of each head...	2	0	0
For the best twenty chilver Down lambs	2	0	0
For the best boar pig of any age	1	0	0
For the best sow pig any age, having mothered a litter	1	0	0
Best pair of young sow pigs, under six months of age	1	0	0

All sheep and pigs to have been bred by the exhibitor.

The sum of £10 for extra stock to be awarded at the discretion of the judges.

PRIZES FOR ROOT CROPS.

A Prize, value £5, given by Joseph Gundry, Esq., for the best three acres of swedes, grown without the application of artificial manure.

A Prize, value £5, given by B. P. Gundry, Esq., for the best five acres of swedes, after a previous green crop.

A Prize, value £5, given by J. A. Damen, Esq., for the best general root crop, not less than 20 acres on the farm.

A Prize, value £5, given by Mr William Way, junr., for four acres of the best common turnips, the manure to have been purchased of him.

A Prize, value £5, given by Mr H. J. Smith, for two acres of the best mangold wurtzel, the manure to have been purchased of him.

For the second best, a Prize value £1.

A Prize, value £5, given by Mr H. J. Smith, for four acres of the best swedes ; the manure to have been purchased of him.

For the second best, a Prize value £1.

Notification of the AGM of the Melplaish (now Melplash) Show to be held on 18 October 1867. As is only to be expected from a Dorset show, sheep were much in evidence in the livestock classes, but the absence of any cattle may cause a few upraised eyebrows.

PRIZES FOR CORN CROPS.

1.—The best sack of white wheat, to be taken from a bulk of not less than twenty sacks—to have been harvested in 1867. ... ...   1 0 0

2.—The best sack of red wheat, to be taken from a bulk of not less than twenty sacks—to have been harvested in 1867. ... ...   1 0 0

3.—The best sack of barley, to be taken from a bulk of not less than twenty sacks—to have been harvested in 1867.... ... ...   1 0 0

PREMIUMS FOR WORK AND SERVICE.

Class 1.—To the man who shall, with reins, plough half an acre of land in the best manner in a given time 2 0 0
    If the plough used be the manufacture of Mr Brown, Melplaish, 10s extra given by him.

Class 2.—To the man, who having at no previous meeting taken a first prize, shall plough with reins, half an acre of land, in the best manner, in a given time 2 0 0
    If the plough used be the manufacture of Mr Brown, 10s extra given by him
    To the second best 1 10 0
    To the third best 1 0 0
    To the fourth best 0 10 0

Class 3.—To the boy not exceeding the age of 17 years, who shall plough half an acre of land, in the best manner, in a given time... ... ...   1 0 0
    To the second best 0 10 0
    To the third best 0 5 0

The sum of £5 given by the Ex-President, Thomas Colfox, Esq., to be awarded at the discretion of the committee, will be distributed thus :—

To the man who shall best double dyke and plush two perches of hedge 1 10 0
    To the second best 1 0 0

To the man who shall best single dyke and plush two perches of hedge 1 10 0
    To the second best 1 0 0

Class 4.—To the male servant in husbandry, who shall have worked the greatest number of years on the same farm, or with the same master, and can produce a certificate of good character 1 0 0
    To the second best 0 10 0

Class 5.—To the female servant in husbandry, who shall have worked the greatest number of years on the same farm, or with the same master, and can produce a certificate of good character 1 0 0
    To the second best 0 10 0

Class 6.—To the servant in husbandry, who shall have brought up the greatest number of legitimate children, in a respectable manner, and with the smallest proportion of parochial relief 1 0 0
    To the second best 0 10 0

The ploughing match will take place in a field at or near Melplaish, where all ploughs intending to compete, must be by 8 o'clock, a.m. The hedgers must be in attendance at the Melplaish Inn, at 7 a m.

No assistance will be permitted to be rendered to the competitors, who must be servants of members of this society.

All stock for exhibition must be on the ground by 10 a m.

All entries must be made on or before the 11th October, at the office of the secretary, either at Bridport, or Beaminster.

Dinner will be provided at Melplaish, at three o'clock, p.m., the President in the chair.

NICHS. M. LOGGIN,
Hon. Sec.

Dated 16th September, 1867.

J.C. & R.H. Palmer's Brewery, West Bay Road, Bridport, 1898. The brewery was founded in 1794 (it celebrates its bi-centenary this year) at the junction of the Brit (seen here) and Asker rivers to the south of the town, Palmer's bought the business one hundred years later.

J.C. & R.H. Palmer's transport in the loading bay at their Old Brewery in South Street, c.1933. The horse-driven dray on the left was almost certainly used for town deliveries.

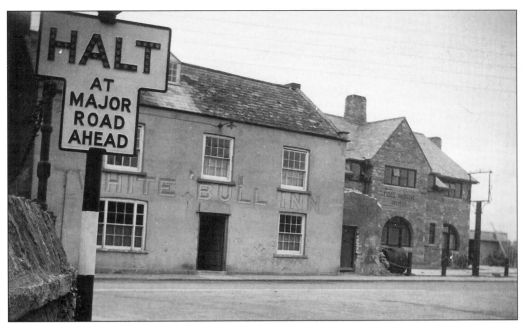

The White Bull Inn, East Road, Bridport, in the 1930s. The inn was demolished around 1940 after the Toll House (the building on the right) had been erected.

The loading bay at J.C. & R.H. Palmer Ltd's brewery in South Street in 1938. Originally a mill, and still possessing the only thatched brewery in England, beer was first brewed here in 1794 by Samual Gundry. The business passed to Mr Job Legg, and was bought by the Palmer family in 1896 and run on their behalf by Mr J.C.Palmer. Today his great-grandsons, John and Cleeves, manage the business which owns almost seventy pubs.

A lorry negotiates the floods at the foot of East Road, Bridport, around 1930. Note the old level crossing gates in the background, where the Bridport branch line crossed the River Asker on its way to West Bay.

The far end of Bridport's East Street, with East Street Station and its thatched station house and level crossing in the distance. The thatched house, which was replaced in 1904, dates the picture to around the turn of the century.

East Street Station, Bridport, c.1901. The thatched station house seen here pre-dated the Bridport branch line's extension to West Bay in 1884. Sadly, perhaps, it was pulled down when the station was rebuilt in 1904.

The West Bay Road roundabout in the 1960s, long before the Bridport bypass was even a twinkle in the planner's eye.

Bridport Town Hall, arguably not the town's most attractive building, dominates by virtue of its very size, most pictures in which it appears; never more so than here, on a market day in around 1914. Brick-built, with Portland stone facings, it was erected in 1785-6 as the Market House on the site of the ancient Chapel of St Andrew, which was thought to have been built in the middle of the 14th century (around 1360). It had been desecrated long before it was pulled down, after, it is said, having been used at various times as a gaol, a Sessions House (with a school overhead) and the chancel used as a clock tower. When the Market House was opened, there were thirty-seven butcher's stalls there, and a smaller building (long since demolished) on the south side contained stalls for corn and produce.

West Street, Bridport, c.1908. The old mill on the left, formerly part of Gundry's, is now David Hedworth, architects.

West Street, Bridport, c.1900. Of interest here are the offices of the *Bridport News*, Bridport's local paper which did not move to its present East Street home until 1965. W. Frost & Co. remained as owners until bought out in 1948, but the shop is still there and still trading as Frosts. Lower down is the Lily Hotel, one of Bridport's best-known inns, which, sadly, closed as recently as January 1994.

West Street, Bridport, c.1905.

West Street, Bridport, at the junction with South Street, c.1905.

West Street, Bridport, after the blizzard of 1891, when Beaminster was cut off for three days. The fact that the only path through the pavement goes to the Royal Oak is purely co-incidental.

West Street, Bridport, 1868. The Sun Inn on the left is now the The Ropemakers Inn.

A. Reynolds' drapers shop in East Street, c.1900. One of Bridport's oldest main street firms, they were established in 1787. Reynolds, who were agents for Pesco Underwear, Singer Sewing Machines and Pullars' Dye Works, and who did all their tailoring and dressmaking on the premises, were also funeral directors. They had a branch at Beaminster (London House). The business finally closed as late as 1955 and the site is now a shopping arcade.

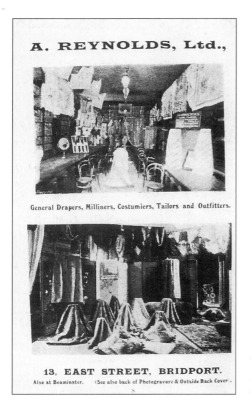

Two interior views of the East Street premises of A. Reynolds Ltd, probably Bridport's leading drapers at the time of the picture in around 1900.

Mrs. A. E. GALE.

Pianos for Hire.

Disc Phonographs.   Cylinder Phonographs.
Latest Records.

SONGS.   MUSIC.

[Registered Design.]

Fancy Goods in Great Variety.
CREST CHINA.   .·.   VIEW GOODS.
PICTURE POSTCARDS.

59 & 61 East St., Bridport.

Mrs Gale's piano shop (mentioned here in a 1905 pocket guide to Bridport) conjures up memories of a bygone – and more genteel – age.

William Elmes, 21 East Street, Bridport, c.1905. Owned by Mr H.P. Castree at the time, Elmes were General and Fancy Drapers and invited residents and visitors to 'pay a visit of inspection… to all departments replete with the latest Novelties'. Today the premises are occupied by Mackays drapery and Theshers Wine Shop.

East Street, Bridport, c.1960, with Humbert's (estate agents) and Green's Garage. Humberts are still there but Green's, who used to serve petrol from pumps on the edge of the pavement, is now Stevenson's Court Flats.

South Street, Bridport, c.1960. Lawrence is now the Black Horse Agencies, the cycle shop is Peach Electric. The archway between the shops led to the old Rope Walks.

Bridport's position as an old coaching call on the London–Exeter run gave it its handsome, wide East Street–West Street main thoroughfare. It also brought increasing traffic problems when the motor car age arrived. The problem, partially cured as recently as the late 1980s by the bypass which loops to the south of the town, was becoming apparent when this picture was taken looking down West Street in around 1935, Smith & Smith, on the left, having moved from South Street in the 1920s.

East Street, Bridport, 1868. The King of Prussia Inn changed its name to The King of Belgians in the same wave of of 'Hun Hating' that, sweeping the country during World War One, swept the British royal family's Saxe-Coburg name into the historical dustbin. Staying with the patriotic theme, and introducing a bit of England into the proceedings, Lord Nelson took over from the Belgian King and remains there to this day. The house to its left was bombed during World War Two and is now the entrance to the East Street car park.

East Street, Bridport, c.1904. Bridport's old post office is on the right; Martin's, the second shop on the left, is now the recently closed Great British Takeaway; the next building is now Barclay's Bank.

No need to worry about passing juggernauts knocking off the handsome gas light attached to
Bridport Town Hall when this picture was taken around 1907. But plenty of horse droppings for
the steam roller to avoid as it makes its stately way up East Street. Today, of course, the lamp
has gone.

The Bull Hotel, East Street, Bridport, c.1910.

East Street, Bridport, c.1903. The Literary and Scientific Institute (now the Dorset County Library), the tall building on the right immediately beyond the ivy-clad house, was formerly known as the Mechanics' Institute, having been established in 1854, the building being given by Mr Henry Warburton, a former Member for Bridport. Apart from a reading room, a collection of curiosities and a circulating library, there were facilities for billiards, chess, draughts, etc. Note the narrower street of the time with the correspondingly wider pavement on the left.

E.C. Hare, East Street, Bridport. The advert was
included in a 1905 Bridport guide.

East Street, Bridport, c.1908. The Bull, Bridport's old coaching hotel, is on the left. The next
shop to it is now Bridget's Market Fruit, next again Granada TV.

Bridport Gas Company shop and works, South Street, c.1908. The manager, James Cornish, is standing in the doorway with his family. The showroom is still standing but is now derelict. The first gasworks in Dorset were at Bridport (c.1832) and the town was the first in the county to use gas for its street lighting. Gas production ceased in 1958.

Floods in Bridport's South Street on 28 November 1929. The archway on the right is the entrance to Market Square The gasworks are behind.

'Tinker' Lee's copper, zinc and tin worker shop, West Street, Bridport, 1898. Later this site became part of the entrance to the Café Royal and the bus depot and car park complex at the bottom of West Street.

The Greyhound Hotel, Bridport, c.1908. The Greyhound's horse bus is on the right.

The Christmas display at T. Norman's butchers shop at 21 South Street, Bridport, about 1905.

Bridport Aeroplane Bank during the Business Men's Week (August 4th-9th 1918), when the town had been asked by the National Committee to purchase £15,000 of War Bonds, the equivalent of buying six aeroplanes. The 'bank' was set up at 26 East Street with all the town's bank managers and the postmaster forming a sub-committee to give assistance. Bridport was justly proud of its magnificent effort in raising no less than £69,070.

East Street, Bridport, c.1930. On the right, the chemists Beach & Company were one of Bridport's oldest main-street firms, having been established in 1788 by G.L. Roberts MD. He ran the business until 1834, it was Beach & Barnicott from 1834-60, James Beach was in charge from 1860-1903, and Mr T.E. Beach took over and was still at the helm at the start of World War Two. Mr Roberts' name was still being retained at the time of this picture, the firm making Dr Roberts' Poor Man's Friend Ointment 'for wounds and skin diseases' and Dr Roberts' Alternative Pills 'for all impurities of the blood'. The latter came in 1/3d, 3s and 5s sizes. On the opposite side of the road, and outside its home base, is the Greyhound Hotel's omnibus that 'met all trains'. Behind it, on the side of the Town Hall's arch, a notice, ' Dangerous Corner On Left', indicates the growing awareness of traffic problems. This, of course, is the South Street junction, long-since guarded by traffic lights.

East Street, Bridport. It is possible to date this picture fairly accurately. Bondfield (see p.11), an early Bridport motoring enthusiast, did not arrive on the extreme right until 1903 and had moved to West Street by around 1908.

South Street, Bridport, c.1900.

South Street, Bridport, c.1930. The Co-op on the right closed in 1993.

South Street, Bridport, c.1908. Both the trees and the outer half of the left hand pavement went in road widening schemes.

South Street, looking south in 1868. Now Bridport's museum, the building centre left was originally built to house a chantry (charity) priest, but it had apparently slid down the social scale by the nineteenth century when it was said to get its 'Castle' name from being a pub of that name. In 1876 a bad fire destroyed the interior. Restored, it became first the Oddfellows' Hall then the Conservative Club. In 1932 the premises were purchased by Capt. Codd and presented to the town as a Museum.

Opposite: The *Bridport News* Printing Works at the rear of Frost's West Street Shop, c.1948. William Charles Frost established a local paper in an office in East Street near the Unitarian Chapel in 1847, eight years before he launched the *Bridport News*. He pioneered the penny newspaper in West Dorset, retiring in 1877 but living to within a few weeks of the paper's 1905 jubilee. The paper stayed in the Frost family's hands until 1948, when Wilfred Frost, a grandson of the founder, retired. The paper moved to West Street in 1862.

Bothen Hood, Bridport, 1944. Today the town has crept much closer to the distinctive hill to the east of Bridport.

Victoria Grove, Bridport, c.1900.

West Allington, Bridport, c.1895. The continuation of West Street, as the main road led out of the town towards Charmouth, Lyme Regis and Axminster, was a part of Bridport little favoured by photographers.

South Street, Bridport, c.1900. The small building in front of the Town Hall was the old fire station.

No. 1 Platoon, E Company, Bridport Home Guard, taken in St Andrews Road around 1941. Front row, left to right: Pte Townsend, Cpl Beale, Cpl Hatton, Sgt Andrews, Mr Nantes, Cpl Bill Foot, Cpl Hansford, Cpl Harwood, Pte Hancock. Others present include Pte Pete Tiltman, two Pte Bullocks, two Pte Bonds (father and son) and Pte Harry Higgins.

Demolishing the railway bridge that once took the branch line over the River Asker into East Street Station and on to West Bay. The bridge was demolished around 1965.

Bridport Station, 1906. The branch line which ran the nine miles from Maiden Newton (on the Yeovil–Weymouth main line) to Bridport was opened on 12 November 1857, a public holiday for the town, with an extension to West Bay coming into use in 1884. Beeching arrived after the extension had been closed in 1964, but the planned 1966 'axing' of the rest of the line was delayed until 3 May 1975.

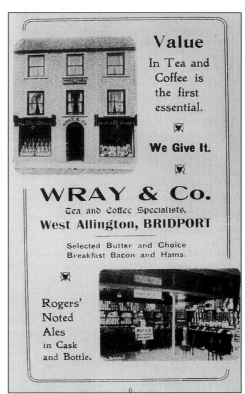

Value In Tea and Coffee is the first essential.

We Give It.

WRAY & Co.
Tea and Coffee Specialists,
West Allington, BRIDPORT

Selected Butter and Choice
Breakfast Bacon and Hams.

Rogers' Noted Ales in Cask and Bottle.

6

Wray & Co, West Allington grocers, c.1905, another advert from a 1905 town guide.

Bridport Infants School, 1898.

West Street, Infant School, on Fire Nov. 12 1906. Bridport.

Bridport's West Street Infants School, also known as Mrs Gundry's School, with its attractive thatch and surrounded on most sides by mill streams, was once an old malt house and said to be over 300 (16th century) years old. It had also served as a pawn store and weaving sheds among other purposes. It became a school in 1838, with Mr Bishop, who formerly had a 'little school' in the King of Prussia Lane, and Mrs Hardy as its first teachers. At the time of the fire (12 November 1906) Miss Dade was the headmistress. The damage was estimated as between £300-400 and, presumably, was paid for by Commercial Union with whom the buildings were insured. The bottom picture shows the school after the fire of 1906.

West Street, Infant School, after the Fire Nov. 12 1906. Bridport

Immediately following the outbreak of World War One, most horses were commandeered by the military authorities. Bridport can be seen here losing much of its 'horse-power' at the collecting point in St Michael's Lane. Exemption was granted to essential animals such as doctors' and farming horses.

A Bridport Market held, unusually, in West Street in 1913.

Bridport Market, West Street, 29 January 1913.

Bridport Market, West Street, 29 January 1913.

Balson & Sons (c.1887), then at No. 7 West Allington, Bridport. William Balson is the small boy in the porch.

In 1890, after changing their trading title to R.J. & W. Balson, Balsons moved a few feet down the road to No. 9, where the butchers business is still in the same family's hands. The baskets on the pavements were used to send meat, via Bridport Station, to Smithfield.

Hussey's bakers shop, West Street, just after the shop was rebuilt in 1950.

R.J. & W. Balson, the West Allington, Bridport butchers shop, in the 1920s, with Richard Balson standing in the porch. Roberts (next door), despite advertising both Rowntree's and Fry's chocolate, made most of the sweets they sold in their sweet factory down the alley seen here between the two shops. Local boys regarded it as a treat to make their way down the alley to the factory and buy a 'hap'oth of damp', half a pound of sweets that had gone soft, for one halfpenny.

The Five Bells, South Street, Bridport, c.1910.

The Ship Inn, South Street, Bridport, 1910. One of the fifteen public houses that could once have been found in the half-mile stretch of South Street between Palmers Brewery and the Town Hall, the Ship is said to have had the first indoor skittle alley in the town. The landlady was Mrs Sarah Beer; her husband ran the saddlers business next door.

Quakers' (Friends') Alms Houses, West Bay Road, Bridport, 1898. Given by Daniel Taylor, a prominent Bridport Quaker, in around 1700, the almhouses were originally a house and tenements in South Street, opposite the parish church. Taylor, a Bridport man born in West Street in a house that stood on the site of today's Gateway supermarket, also provided the Quaker following with a nearby barn to convert into a meeting place.

The Bridport Arms, West Bay, c.1933.

The Parade, West Bay, c.1903. The year 1385 probably saw the beginning of Bridport Harbour; in that year John Hudresfield undertook to make a harbour 'where there was previously none', provided he was allowed to levy a halfpenny for every horseload of saleable goods imported or exported for a term of three years. Prior to that there are grounds to suppose that small boats came up the Brit towards Bridport itself.

West Bay, c.1910, before any development began on the west side of the village where the old golf course was situated. Later the course was moved to the opposite side of West Bay (East Cliff) where the Bridport and West Dorset Golf Club and its Bogey-73 18-hole course enjoyed a particularly fine reputation in the 1920s and '30s.

West Bay, around 1930, with the fields in the background behind the River Brit packed with tents.

The pleasure steamer *Victoria* at West Bay around 1930. This popular steamer plied between Weymouth and Torquay and called at West Bay en route. It was also a regular at West Bay Regatta, where it gave excursions in the bay for a sixpenny fare.

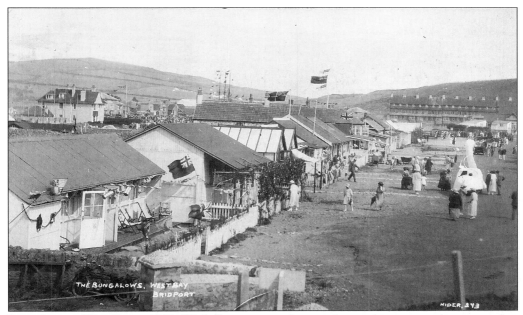

Bungalows at West Bay, c.1922. With flags very much in evidence, this seems to be regatta day, especially given the flag-decked masts of the ship in the centre background and the crowd to the left.

Decorated boats on the River Brit during a West Bay Regatta around 1910.

Whit Tuesday Fair, West Bay, 1860. John Cox's ship-building yards are in the right hand background beside the harbour. Formerly shipbuilding was an important industry at West Bay; vessels as large as the *Speedy* (1,002 tons and launched in 1856) and the *Nourmahal* (846 tons in 1859) were built there, but the industry ended with the launching of the *Lilian* in 1879.

The Mound, West Bay, c.1920. There was a pierrot show here (at the Pavilion) before and after World War One and, at the time, the tea rooms on the left were a favourite haunt for the local boys, with hot Oxo a favourite drink. Around 1924 the tea rooms were washed out to sea and today the harbourmaster's office stands on the site.

Bridport (West Bay) Harbour, 1835.

West Bay Harbour, c.1950.

The Russian vessel *Nerne* unloading hemp for Bridport's rope industry in 1908.

West Bay Station, seen here shortly after the branch line was extended to Bridport's Harbour in 1884. The line was closed between 1915-19 for wartime economy reasons Increased competition from coach companies led to its closing to passenger services in 1930, but goods traffic contined to use the line until 1962.

The Roller Skating Rink at Walditch, near Bridport, c.1909. The rink is in use today as a real tennis court.

The Coastguard (left) and railway stations at West Bay, c.1905.

E.Holborrow, in his home-made boat, before leaving West Bay to cross the Atlantic Ocean on 11 July 1914. Holborrow, who was disabled, made his boat at Burton Bradstock Cliffs with a knife and a saw, launching it at Burton Bradstock before sailing to Bridport Harbour (West Bay), where it stayed for a year while he made various additions. During that year he slept out on the cliffs in a waterproof sleeping bag. Not unnaturally, he made the national press, especially when he ran into difficulties in the Channel and was towed into Plymouth, where the vessel was visited by thousands of people and it was discovered that he had only half a sovereign (50p) and supplies for 100 days.

Two
Bridport and its Harbour
The People

A Bridport postman on his rounds in the 1880s. Note both the boots and gaiters and his four long-service stripes on his tunic.

This card was sent to 19727 Sapper Brooks of the 55th Field Company (Royal Engineers) at Roberts Heights, Pretoria, on 6 June 1912 by his wife (?) Annie from 8 Rope Walks. On it she tells him that it is 'the Church School boys going to the Picture Palace on Empire Day. The Mayor (Mr Luttrill) treated them.' The Bridport Electric Palace (in Barrack Street and formerly the Liberal Hall) became the Lyric Cinema and today houses the Bernard Gale School of Dancing.

Like the cards opposite, this is another Sapper Roberts card. It shows the then new Artillery Barracks in St Michael's Lane, Bridport, seen here in 1912. Today it houses the Youth Club.

St Mary's School Treat procession on 23 June 1910 making its way along East Street. Mrs Roberts has marked herself with an 'X', and goes on tell her husband that her friend Ethel is behind her but hidden by a flag. Her husband was still in England at the time and stationed at Brompton Barracks in Chatham.

Black is much in evidence in 1910, with Bridport in mourning for Edward VII's death. This card shows the Memorial Service procession making its way down South Street towards St Mary's church. Presumably Sapper Roberts was an old scout as his wife is at pains here to tell him that 'we now have nearly 30 Boy Scouts', most of whom seem to be out of step with the rest of the parade.

Wilson Hansford, van driver for the West Street bakers Roberts & Sons, poses with his Ford van around 1918.

Staff at Bridport Grammar School, June 1927. Staff (in the second row back, left to right) are: Mr Alston (Science), Mr Taylor (History and Geography), Miss Broughton (English), Miss Bickford (Science and Maths), Mr Hill (Headmaster and English), Miss Witham (French), Miss Owen (French), -?- (Art), Mr Telford (Latin and History). The head boy, Syd Phillips, is behind the Headmaster. On his right is the head girl, a Miss Davey, on his left the three prefects, Fred Meech, Bill Kingman and Bill Loveford.

Charles William Groves jun., middleman in five generations of a Piddletrenthide family that moved their market gardening business from Dorchester to Bridport in 1936. It was in 1866 that the first Charles William Groves decided to give up selling bibles and grow plants, mainly for the production of seed, in a nursery at Piddletrenthide. He was followed in the business by his son, another Charles William, and the C.W. Groves & Son trading title, still in use today, was born. Two other Charles William Groves followed in turn, and today the fifth generation of the family keeps the by-now traditional C.W. initials, albeit as Clive Watt, a habit passed on to the sixth generation in his two sons. The firm, among the pioneers in Britain of the production of onion sets in the 1930s, can provide most plants, but specialises in violets, the latter being sent as far afield as Canada and Japan.

Bridport Station, c.1905.

Bridport branch line's centenary celebrations in 1957 included the posing of Bridport Station staff for a group picture. Back row, left to right: J. Marsh, W. Knoakes, R. Williams, J. Crichard, S. Burnett, ? Chard. Middle: F. James, W. Hunt, L. Coombes, P. Miller, W. 'Chalky' White, J. Bonney, R. England, C. Latham, C. Belben, Mr Cousins, J. Edmunds, T. Station, J. Ward, E. Burgoyne, C. Vennel, R. Pavey, Mr Poole. Front: R. Foster, J. Dean, C. Sansom, Mr Sheppard, Miss Jean Hawkins, R. Dimmick, Mr Gover (station master), Mr Rendell, J. Martin, Mr Darby, R. Brown, D. Legg.

R. J. Balson's delivery 'boy' Roy Travers, with the motor cycle's answer to the errand boy's bike around 1930. The sidecar, seen here parked on the opposite side of West Street to the Lily Hotel, had been known to bring a certain well-known Bridport butcher home from school on a rainy day! Balson's claim 'Quick Service' here. They could well have added 'long-established', the family being in butchering in Bridport at least as long ago as Henry VIII's reign (1509-47), when a John Balson was in business with a shambles in South Street. Twenty-five reigns later, if you include both Oliver and Richard Cromwell, they are still in Bridport. We know that in 1825 Henry Balson had stall number eleven in the new Town Hall (opened 1786), and a brother (?), Joseph, had number twenty. Possibly two other brothers, Henry at the Plymouth Inn and William at the Kings Arms, were innkeepers but later went back to butchering, and it is from that line of the family that the present generations descend. Some years ago a challenge was made in a butchering journal to any family butchers that could beat the Balson record. There were no takers.

Comic Football at Bridport Cricket & Lawn Tennis Club's ground around 1921. Richard Balson is third from the left in front. Behind the pavilion, which survived until after World War Two, can be seen Palmers' brewery.

Before the two companies amalgamated, an annual football match between the rival Bridport net manufacturing firms, Edwards and Gundrys, was always a keen affair. Here the 1952 Edwards team is, rear row, left to right: Des O'Connor, Joe White, Archie Greenham, Bill Croad, -?-, Fred Verymn. Front: Reg Tuck, Doug Pinkett, John Kearns, Len Follett, L.Hansford.

Bridport Football Club, 1912-13. Back row, left to right: Roy Frost, J. Balson, A. Andress. Middle: C. Hardy, J. Knight, A. Bolt, ? Stembridge, -?-. Front: the Revd Mr Brazier (Bridport's vicar), Bob Ash, Jim Hanson.

Old Brewery (Palmers) tug-of-war team, 1911-12. The board says they won first prize, but not where or what. What is certain is that they trained on Palmers!

Bridport Cricket Club 1st XI, c.1952. Back row, left to right: Frank Hibbert (umpire), Mike Brake, Brian Roper, Bert Cordier, Vernon Payne, Frank Wright, Ernest Choldcroft (scorer). Front: Derek Callam, Brian Saunders, Mart Radcliffe, Derek Gale (capt.), Dave Cox, Bill Graves.

Bridport Congregational Church Harvest Festival, 2 March 1917, showing the Revd W.L. Brown and Mrs Brown (both on the extreme right) with helpers at a time when harvest festivals throughout the land directed their attentions to helping war works, especially hospitals.

Bridport Scout Troop, c.1910. Bridport's vicar, the Revd Mr Brazier, is the scout master in the middle of the seated row.

Bridport Scouts and Cubs, c.1925. The Revd Mr Brazier is the scout master and Mr Dinham his assistant; among the scouts are Fred Tutton, Bill Kingman, Hussey, Biles, George Corrick (whose family ran the local jam factory), Ivan Bowen, George Hussey and Lloyd Burwood.

West Allington School, 1933. Among the pupils are Cyril Tiltman, Les Berry, Doug Langley, Raymond Stickley, Ron Day, Harry Fenwick, Joan Hussey, Austin Baker, Bill Taylor, Gilbert White, Eileen Hocking, Ida Rendell and Phylis Chard. The headmaster, Mr J. Walker, is in the left background, Miss Ball, a teacher, to the right.

William Edward Randall, who was born at Loders in 1847, was Mayor of Bridport in 1899 and 1910, and is seen here at his home at 12 South Street. He attended Bridport Boys General School, where John Beard was headmaster for forty years (1854-94), and became a pupil teacher. Later in life he took over the Wine & Spirit Shop in South Street (now The Book Shop) from W.H. Chick. He took his council and mayoral duties seriously, to the extent of riding around the town spotting litter and issuing orders for its removal. Looking at his own and the horse's immaculate turn-out (note the polished or painted hooves), this is not hard to accept.

Bridport Church of England School, Class Three, 1915. The class mistress is Miss Spencer.

Bridport Church of England School Infants Class, 1915. Among the pupils are: Jack Leaker, Bill Kingman, ? Gillingham, Frank Allen, ? Tuck, Lloyd Hicks, Ernie Hansford, ? Phillips and Eli Clark.

Bridport (and District) Cricket Club vs MCC, 1898. Back row, left to right: F.J.Hutchings (sec), ? Phillips, G.T. Metcalfe, E.W. Hirst, ? Tyler, Capt. Kindersley, J.N. Williams, ? Woodcock, W.H. Price, J. Vesey, Mr Moss (umpire). Middle: the Revd Mr Jephson, Dr Kitson, the Revd Mr Kindersley, the Revd Mr Farrar (the Bridport skipper), H.H. Palairet (MCC skipper), L.C.H. Palairet, R.N.C. Palairet, F.C. Bond, the Revd Mr Knott. Front: A. Zealley, R. Dewdney, J. Zeally, ? Carlin, ? Watts. One can only assume that where the players' surnames only are given they are professionals and thus not worthy of initials. The Bridport cricket club was formed in 1885 and played on a ground at Pymore until 1909, when a move to the Brewery ground was made. The pavilion seen here was taken to the new ground.

Mr H.R.C. Palmer lays the foundation stone of the Toll House Inn in 1938. Legend has it that many of the stones used here came from the old brewery at Netherbury (see p. 100).

The Peace Thanksgiving Service outside Bridport's Town Hall. Although the card has 1918 written on the back, it is more likely to be 1919, when hostilities officially ceased. This seems to be borne out by the rows of obviously ex-servicemen in 'civvies'.

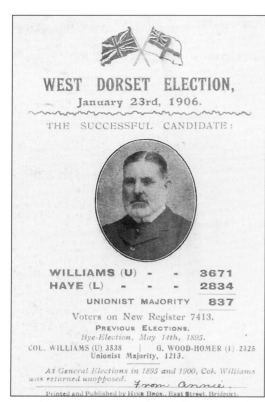

Col. R. Williams, the successful Unionist candidate for West Dorset in the 1906 General Election. First returned after a by-election in May 1895, Williams was returned unopposed after a general election later the same year and again in 1900.

Workers at Brit Engineering around 1910.

Hussey's bakehouse, West Street, c.1950, with the firm's first electric delivery van on the right. Arthur Baker (left) and Gilbert Staple are unloading eggs and placing them in water glass.

The Kings Arms Barrel Club Annual Dinner at Allington (Bridport) Parish Hall, 26 January 1952. Guest of honour at the top table is Mr H.R.C. Palmer. With him are the following officers: W.S. Gale (President), A.S. Gale (chairman), F. Smith (treasurer), and F.A. Webb and B.E. Williams (joint secretaries).

Melplash Show, c.1955. Bill Kingman, centre, show assistant secretary for thirty-three years (1927-60), poses with his successor, Mr Pern, on his left, and the chairman, Mr Bishop, on his right. Mrs Ascot, owner of the recently demolished West Mead Hotel, is on the extreme left.

Bridport Boys School. Mr Mashes' class's 1957 production of *Lady Dorothy Dangerfield*. Back row, left to right: Graham Elliott, -?-, Gerald Watts, Victor Williams, Mark Lewis, Clive Groves, Paul Bryant, Rex Bale, Richard Brooks, -?-, -?-. Front: Michael Turner, Michael Lister, Gregory Cox, Ben Sill, John Hallett, Ben Jones, Roy Cumming, John Sill, Barry Bevis, -?-, -?-.

Bridport Ancient Order of Foresters on an outing to Cheddar in the early 1920s in one of Bondfield's charabancs. Leonard Gale from Powerstock in on the extreme right.

Bert Budden (centre) and Godfrey 'Goff' Crabb, who worked as a hairdresser at Stan Gale's barbers shop in West Street, on his left, are among the passengers seen here at Bournemouth, in a charabanc belonging to the Bluebird Company, who used to operate from premises where the Somerfield supermarket now stands. Tickets for the steamship *Victoria* (see p.52) could be purchased at Sydenham's booking office in the background.

Lady members of the Congregational Church in East Street pictured prior to their departure on an outing to an unknown destination around 1921. The building in the left background is the Literary and Scientific Institute, which survives today as the local branch of the Dorset County Library. Restricted to 12 m.p.h. as these charabancs were, imagine the duration of what could at best be described as a bumpy journey to, say, Cheddar, a popular destination at the time.

Three
Beaminster, Netherbury, Melplash and Stoke Abbott

Ross Marks haymaking with real horse-power at Slape Manor, Netherbury, c.1947.

The Market House Inn, Beaminster Square, 1850. Beaminster was granted a market by Edward I in 1284, and although it is not known when a market house was first built an earlier one had been destroyed by fire in 1781. The building shown here, which replaced it and had butchers shambles on the left, was pulled down in 1868.

Hogshill Street, Beaminster, 1902. The New Inn certainly existed as early as 1754, but was closed in the 1930s. Today Bugler's Showrooms occupy the site.

Beaminster Market around the turn of the century, and certainly after 1868, as the old Market House (see opposite) stood here until then.

Beaminster Square, c.1933.

Looking into Beaminster's Fleet Street from the Square, c.1902.

St Mary Well Street, Beaminster, c.1912. St Mary Well Street, which led to the old gasworks (closed around 1982), was formerly known as Duck Street because of the stream that flowed down it (and the ducks that lived there). When the gasworks were built in 1860 the stream was diverted.

Thomas Pine's grocery shop, Beaminster, c.1907.

Hann's Garage, Prout Bridge, Beaminster, c.1935. Arthur Bullock is serving petrol. Going out of sight in the background, Harold Wakely of Cherry Cot Farm is doing his milk round.

BEAMINSTER
Peace Day Celebrations
JULY 19th, 1919.

Committee.

Rev. W. V. JEPHSON (Chairman). Mr. E. B. STOKES (Hon. Treas.)
Mr. F. BUGLER (Hon. Sec.)

Mrs. Rhodes Moorhouse,
Rev. Canon Hutchings,
Major G. A. Pinney,
Capt. G. A. Scutt,
Mr. J. Rogers,
Mr. Fred C. Poole,
Mr. Van H. Allen,
Mr. Henry Crocker,
Mr. F. Andress,
Mr. J. F. Pile,
Mr. C. Battrick.

Miss Wills,
Miss Ward,
Mrs. Dicker,
Mr. L. Skeym,
Mr. C. Collins,
Mr. B. V. Johnson,
Mr. W. L. Sherring,
Mr. Robert Hine,
Mr. B. B. Ryall,
Mr. R. Dunell.

PROGRAMME.

The Inhabitants of the Town are asked to decorate their houses by 9 a.m.

The Ringers will give Peals on the Bells during the day.

The Beaminster Brass Band will be in attendance all day.

Tea for Children under 15 will be given by the Comrades of the Great War, in the Public Hall at 5 p.m.

The Manor House Grounds have been thrown open to the Public by T. W. RUSSELL, Esq., from 2.30 p.m. onwards.

The Inhabitants of Mapperton are invited to join with Beaminster.

Dancing 7—10.   Grand display of Fireworks 10 p.m.

BONFIRE.

V. H. Allen, Printer and Photographer, Beaminster.

Beaminster Peace Day Celebrations, 19 July 1919. The day began at 10.30 with the assembly of all units prior to the arrival of Sir Reginald Pinney KCB, who was to inspect the troops and present medals before the march-past. Afterwards, and before an afternoon of sports, a captured German gun was handed over to the town.

Assembling horses in Beaminster Square for compulsory purchase by the military authorities at the start of World War One.

Unveiling of War Memorial Gun, Beaminster, 2 January 1921. The gun, captured from the Germans in France, stood on a plinth of local stone and had the names of the 325 men of the town who had served in World War One carved in Ham stone on its side. It was unveiled by Air Marshall Sir Hugh Trenchard, and it was said at the time that 'it will remain for many generations to come', but it actually went for scrap twenty years later during World War Two; the plinth stayed on until the 1960s, by which time it had become a traffic hazard and was removed, the portion with the names on being placed in the wall outside St Mary's church. The gun was presented to Beaminster in recognition of the bravery of Lt. W.B.R. Moorhouse from nearby Parnham House, the first airman to win the Victoria Cross.

Beaminster Bellringers outside St Mary's church after ringing a peal on Queen Elizabeth II's Coronation Day, 2 June 1953. They include Cecil Poole, Ted Bailey, Bill Bailey, Joe Barrett and Frank Brooks.

Beaminster Football Club, 1937-38, the season the club were Dorset Intermediate Cup winners, beating Portland Red Triangle 3-1 in the final. Back row, left to right: Doug Perkins, ? Park, Arthur Bugler, Fred Trump, George Hunt, Arthur 'Bob' Mason. Middle: Herbert Watts, Fred Lumbard, John Cleal, Fred Watts, Gordon Willey. Front: Len Marsh, Ron Gill.

John Hunt's 'Beaminster Bus' outside Hunts Steam Sawmills and Carriage Accessories at Southgate, Beaminster, in 1902. The prototype 'BRIT' was a modified Daimler, designed by John Hunt (at the wheel with John Goodland standing on the right), and had a replacement engine and gearbox manufactured by E.A. Chard & Co. of Bridport (later to become Brit Engineering Works Ltd). A few other cars were built and sold locally; this one, which was registered in 1904 with an FX94 number, was used to give visitors penny trips around the town. It is said, although no one knows where, that its engine is buried in the grounds behind. There is an amusing story connected with Dorset car registration numbers. Originally the prefix BF was allocated to the county; for obvious reasons there was an outcry, and the numbers were changed to FX!

Staff at Beaminster & Netherbury Grammar School, c.1928. Left to right: Mr Mussel, Miss Peters, Mr Skyrm (head), Miss Hann, Mr Habbitts, Miss Hastings, Mr Graveson.

The Half Moon, Melplash, c.1905. Of interest to the modern generation will be the long since gone ivy on the still popular inn.

The old blacksmith's forge and workshop, Melplash, c.1903. As a different kind of horse power began to take over, these premises were turned into a garage, and in 1951 became the Melplash Motors still there today (see p. 90).

Melplash, c.1900. The blacksmith's shop (above) is in the background. Gappers, the left hand cottage, is no longer there, but Grooms Cottage, on the right, still stands.

Schoolchildren at Melplash, c.1901.

George Mears, with his wife Mary, at the wheel of his home-made racing car in August 1957. The car had been converted from a 1936 Austin van and its body was made of exceptionally light aluminium. In its first race, at the West Hants and Dorset Car Club's meeting at Ibsley, the car came second. George Mears, who began his working life at Powerstock Mill, became one of the best-known men in the West Dorset garage world after beginning his own Melplash Motors business in 1951.

Pitchers, Salway Ash, with the Anchor Inn in the background, in 1926.

An all-male outing in one of Bondfield's (Bridport) charabancs photographed before setting off to an unknown destination from the Blue Ball at Dottery (see p.94). Among those standing are Mr Sorson, Alf and Fred Chubb, George Slade, George Hansford and the landlord Mr Blair (next to driver). Those inside include Albert, Syd and Eli Spiller and George Chubb.

A Salway Ash Panto Players production at the village school, c.1952. Among those taking part are Pamela Scaddings, Doris Patten, Christine Bagwell, June Sturmey, Jim Gurd, Peggy Bennett, Janet and Valerie Slade, and Barbara, Sylvia and Mrs Spencer.

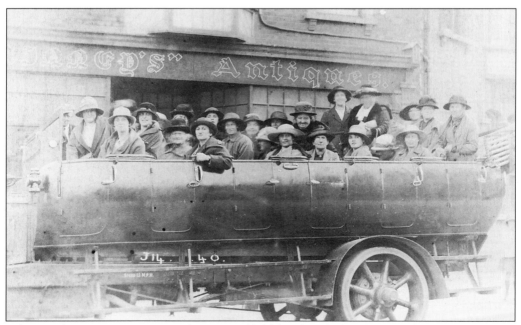

Salway Ash WI outing to Exmouth in a Bondfield (Bridport) charabanc in the early 1920s. Mrs Cox and Mrs Shapcott are among members seen here.

Almost the entire village, with a few from Broadoak and Watton to make up the numbers, are off on a Salway Ash outing to Southsea around 1947.

Salway Ash football team, c.1921. Back row, left to right: Alfie Williams, Jack Chubb, -?-, Fred Pinkett, Percy Gale, Len Giles, -?-. Bill Slade is on the right of the front row; Miss 'Girlie' Record sits in front.

The Blue Ball Inn, Dottery, between Bridport and Salway Ash (c.1928), now, sadly, one of many pubs closed in the area.

Netherbury Sunday School outing, prior to leaving from outside the old chapel in the Square, in coaches belonging to the Beaminster-based Gibbs coach firm, c.1948. Among the happy faces can be seen Deirdre Wakley, Archie, Nita, June and Jean Pye, Denise and Roger Dowle, Doug Spencer, John and Tony Hallett, Robert Moores, Ken Bullock, Rosemary Russell, Mrs Mollie Russell and Hilda Moores.

Netherbury Football Club, 1950-51. Back row, left to right: Cyril Chapman, Geoff Martin, Bert Gay, Ron Winters, ? Chapman, Tony Hallett, George Hawkins, Pete Mason, Graham Moores, Frank Dawe, Jimmy Pye, Alfie Lansam. Front: Ted Mallows, Joe Chubb, Ken Bullock, Arthur Smith, Joe Crichard.

Netherbury Football Club, c.1958-59. Back row, left to right: Bill Gay, Arthur Lawrence, Bobby Hodder, Brian Hawkins, Stuart Dowle, Ron Gurd, John Way, Tony Spencer. Front: Gordon Legg, ? Matterface, Andrew Dowle, Roger Dowle, Jack Gardner.

Voluntary labour preparing the Tower Hill site of Netherbury's War Memorial around 1920.

Dedication of Netherbury War Memorial, c.1921.

An event at Netherbury Reading Room, still very much in use today, around 1928. Among those present are Bill Lewis, Charles Lewis, Archie Pye, Bert Walker, Bill Stevens and Jessie Davis.

Apart from Bert Walker at the back, and the gent in front, this appears to be the ladies 'half' of the occasion in the picture above at Netherbury Reading Room. Among those seen are Rebecca Stone (village shopkeeper), Margorie Moores, Francis Pye and Ethel Hallett. Laura Lacey, left in the seated row, who lived next door to the Star Inn, was the seventh daughter of a seventh daughter and a fortune-teller of great repute in the district.

New Inn Street, Netherbury, seen here around 1906, took its name from the New Inn on the left. Both the inn and the houses opposite were later destroyed by fire.

The Brandon Hotel, Netherbury, seen here around 1910, closed as recently as 1984, when Ken Dowle was the last landlord. This popular inn had been in the Dowle family's hands for over eighty years at the time. At the turn of the century an Albert Dowle had been landlord of the New Inn at the rear of the Brandon; and it was at that time that the licence was transferred to the Brandon.

The Star Inn, Netherbury, 1953, with Charlie Wakley, landlord for sixteen years at the time. Sadly, the pub, which stood next to the old village brewery, has since closed and is now derelict.

Miss Blair's Choral Class, in the now closed Netherbury Village Hall, c.1922. Back row, left to right: Sybil Martin, Nina Stevens, Marion Moores, Ida Whitemore, Mrs Lacy, Mrs D. Hallett, Gladys Dryden, Hilda Woodbury, Nurse Stevens, Mrs Smith, Mrs Stone (village shop), Mrs Hann, Ciss Woodland, Cissie Hallett. Front: Faith Stone, Edna Lawrence, Mrs Bailey, Mrs Carter, Miss Blair, Francis Lewis, Nellie Lawrence, Miss Fry.

Netherbury, c.1905. The tall chimney visible in the background belonged to Legg's Brewery. It was pulled down between the two wars and much of the material went to build the Toll House Inn at Bridport.

Netherbury British Legion (the Royal came later) at a supper in the Village Hall, c.1949. Seated are, left to right: George Hawkins, Bert Walker, Ken Dowle, Billy Griffin, -?-, -?-, Bert Marks, -?-, -?-.

Netherbury Militia at the Star Inn, c.1914. Alb Dowle is second from the left.

Netherbury School, c.1956. Mrs Mabel Bailey (headmistress) is on the extreme right, Miss Hinton half hidden on the left. Among pupils of the school, which closed in 1974, are Brian and Elaine Tither, Stuart and Andrew Dowle, Ted Willmot, Ed Woodbury, Graham and Brian Hawkins, Stuart Gay, Barbara Leach, Nigel Pye, Edna Gundry and Teresa Dunsbury.

High Street, Netherbury, c.1895, since renamed St James Road.

WI Outing, Netherbury, c.1926. Standing at back, left to right: Mrs Collins, Miss Chubb, Mrs Denner, Mrs Moores. Sitting: Miss Dunham, Mr Puckess (the driver, and looking singularly unconcerned at the prospect of driving the ladies on their outing), Marion Moores, ? Lewis, Mrs B. Hodder, Mrs Turner, Mrs Lacy, Miss Chubb, Mrs Beat Watts and Mrs Dowle. John Stone is standing on the extreme left.

Bridge Street, Netherbury, c.1907. The village stores on the right has long since closed, leaving Netherbury without a single shop.

Netherbury Post Office, c.1910, at the entrance to High (now St James) Street. The part building on the right was the old chapel which was later used as a mill and has been a private workshop since 1948.

Stoke Abbott, 1910.

The Star Inn, Bridge Street, Netherbury, c.1905.

Stoke Abbott, c.1900. There is a fine country church here which numbers the poet Crowe among its former rectors. The church was partially rebuilt after the tower was struck by lightning in 1828, and almost completely rebuilt fifty years later.

The old chapel, Waytown, seen here around the turn of the century but long since demolished and rebuilt as a private house.

The Hare and Hounds, Waytown, c.1905.

Bill Chubb, a blacksmith and wheelwright whose craft was well known far beyond the confines of his workshop here in the Marshwood Vale at Broadoak, at work around 1885.

Four

Bothenhampton, Burton Bradstock, Shipton Gorge, Loders and Askerswell

The old cyder house and granary (seen here in 1930) which was converted in 1932 in to Bothenhampton Men's Club.

Lower High Street, Burton Bradstock, c.1905, with thatch much in evidence.

Burton Bradstock, 1902.

Burton Bradstock.

High Street, Burton Bradstock, c.1909. The tall wall to the right of the Anchor Inn is still there, albeit much improved and with window added.

BURTON BRADSTOCK, BRIDPORT.

Greenwich Cottage, Burton Bradstock, c.1935. Cheney's Garage (now Burton Bradstock Motors) is on the left. Much of this area has been prone to flooding from the nearby River Bride, the cottage itself has been often submerged to the eaves, and the road, where it runs out of our picture on the right towards Weymouth, had to be raised four feet for some distance.

Shadrack, Burton Bradstock, 1928. Cattle belonging to local farmer and butcher Rodney Gale are brought home for milking.

Mill Street, Burton Bradstock, c.1938. The post office, seen here to the left of the Three Horseshoes Inn, moved in post-war years to the first of the houses beyond the pub.

Bridge Cottage Stores, High Street, Burton Bradstock, c.1933. The village takes its name from *Brideton* (settlement on the Bride) and Bradenstock (the Wiltshire abbey to which it once belonged).

The beach at Burton Bradstock, c.1920. Note the old coast road climbing over the headland towards West Bay.

The junction of Chapel Street and Shadrack, Burton Bradstock, c.1910. This pretty village, which has far more than its fair share of thatch, was once the home of the Roberts family, a member of which was Nelson's clerk at Trafalgar.

A 'mobile bazaar', laden down with almost everything a household needs, makes a sale in Burton Bradstock around 1935.

VE Day celebrations in Bothenhampton's main street in May 1945. The tall wall behind the children belonged to the stables (towards the left) and the barns of Manor Farm. Now demolished, the site has been redeveloped.

Bothenhampton Men's Club outing in 1933. The first outing organised by the club, it took members to Bournemouth via Corfe Castle, Swanage and the Studland ferry. Back row, left to right: Cecil Cleall, Tom Meach, Bill Hix, Dick Rawles, Fred Scovell, Bill King, Walter Russell, Bill Cleall, John Hoskins, Friedland Lankshear, Lloyd Hix (now in his 80s, and the only surviving member of the group). Front: Freddie Gale, Bert Legg, Charles Saunders, Ernie Hix, Charles Goddard, Albert Ash, George Goddard.

Church Street, Bothenhampton (c.1920), looking up from the village towards the buildings destroyed by fire in 1925.

On 9 June 1925 this handsome row of cottages in Church Street, Bothenhampton was destroyed by fire. After making the mile-long journey from their station, Bridport Fire Brigade were only able to run one hose to the fire, and that only after damming a stream. With so little water and the cottages already largely destroyed, they concentrated on damping down the thatch of the house opposite.

114

Sundown, Bothenhampton, c.1936, with Ethel Hamblin (left) and Walter Saunders outside. Although much of the wall and hedge has gone, and the door has grown a porch, the iron railings surprisingly survived the various World War Two salvage drives.

Bothenhampton School, Group II, 1921. Back row, left to right: -?-, Gillingham, Watts, Mary Holt, Rhoda Hughes, Dorothy Gerrard, Gilbert Gerrard, Miss Shilton (headmistress). Middle: Watts, -?-, -?-, Veronica Varndell. Front: Gillingham, Nora Hoare, Philip Saunders, Edna Smith, Stanley Smith, Rhoda Jeanes (Rhoda was from one of the families made homeless after the fire in Church Street (see opposite) and she returned to the school for temporary accommodation).

Mr R.C. Palmer (centre) shakes hands with Mr Atkins (landlord) at the opening of the skittle alley at the now closed George Inn, Bothenhampton, in around 1960. Mrs Atkins is on the right.

Bothenhampton School shortly before its closure in 1923, when the pupils were transferred to Bridport. Back row, left to right: Miss Shilton (headmistress), Veronica Varndell, Gilbert Gerrard, Jeanes, Jack Ash, Jeanes, Tom Hughes, -?-, Tim Gillingham, Ted Hughes, George Gillingham. Middle: Leslie Smith, Eric Ashton, Walter Saunders, Bill Varndell, Philip Saunders, Dorothy Gerrard, Rhoda Hughes, Mary Holt, -?-. Front: Dennis Watts, Peter Miller, Varndell, Hughes, Jack Holt, Clifford Udall, Travers, George Jeanes, Audrey Herring.

The Travellers Rest, Shipton Gorge, c.1920. This old pub was once a Bridport receiving house, a place where letters could be left for collection by the postal authorities on a regular basis.

The old porch (see above) at the Travellers Rest, Shipton Gorge (c.1930), complete with well and seats where, in fine weather, would-be passengers waited for the coach.

Shooting party outside the Travellers Rest, c.1914. Bob Fooks is on the right. One can only assume that the postman (complete with two long-service bars on breast pocket) had only stopped to check the quality of the cyder jar!

A council road-making gang on the main Dorchester road between Bridport and the Travellers Rest around 1913. Today, of course, this is the busy main A35 trunk road. Left to right: -?-, -?-, -?-, Eddie Fooks, George Marsh, Mark Fooks, -?-.

Albert John Wells, seen here with his champion Landrace sow and the Christopher Hill Cup for most points in the pig classes at the 1951 Melplash Show, was born at Pembroke Dock. He moved first to Bradpole, then Bothenhampton, from where he travelled to work for the Bridport butcher Mr Fletcher. He left in 1939 to start his own butchers business in Loders (where his wife was postmistress for many years), continuing there until his death in 1968; shortly afterwards his son Robin moved to Bridport's South Street where he continues in business today. Albert Wells, an inspector in the Special Constabulary, took a keen interest in local markets and fatstock shows, at which he was a well-known and highly respected judge, between Exeter and Dorchester.

Children's Fancy Dress at Loders House in about 1945, judging by the 'This is What Our Heroes Expect To Come Home To' placard on the right. Children, left to right: one Ostler twin, Robin Wells, Tom Yarde, Dave Crabb, Margaret Barnes (back), Christine Harris, Wendy Richards, the other Ostler twin.

Loders Home Guard, 1941. Back row, left to right: Ptes Ward, Legg, Paul, Bourne, Read, Saunders, Nobbs, Glyde, Darby, Darby. Middle: Ptes Osborne, Gurd, Bennett, Hyde, Taylor, Walker, Collier, Crabb, Tucker, Crabb. Front: Cpl Chester, Sgt H. Tucker, Sgt A. Budden, Capt. G. Wellstead, Col. Sir E.P. Le Breton, Sgt A. Wells, Cpl Wrixon, Cpl Shelton. The Boy Scout in front, probably used as a messenger, is Wilf Crabb.

William and Isobel Bridge with their family at Loderland Farm, c.1909. Children, left to right: William Leslie, Cecil Herbert, Ivy Muriel, Florence Isobel.

Procession on route to a pageant at Loders Court, c.1910. George Randall is in the foreground. Note the Yonderover Bridge in the background, which took the Bridport branch line over the Uploders Road at that point.

Outside one of the barns at Upton Manor Farm, Uploders, c.1912. Left to right: George Randall, Arthur Hansford, Alf Crabb, Jim Hawker, Eddie Hansford, George Hawker and Edwin Edward Randall, the farmer.

Loders Church Choir, c.1908. Back row only, left to right: Revd D. Thomas, Millicent Crabb, Ella Randall, Frances Curtis. Jessie Row, Gladys Blackler, Gladys Brown, Hilda Russell, Miss Thomas.

Loders Women's Institute 'Tea Ladies' at Loders Fête, c.1910. Front row, left to right: Mrs W. Brown, Miss Lockwood, Mrs Greening, Mrs Jesse Hansford, Mrs Edwin Randall, Mrs Knight. Front: Sarah Ann Travers, Mrs Pitcher, Mrs Crabb, Mrs May Samways, Beattie Clark, Ethel Howe.

Symondsbury, c.1905.

Committee members of Askerswell & District Young Farmers Club at the Harvest Supper, 1951. Left to right: Mary Foot, Alan Musgrove, Margorie Randall, Edgar Bishop, Clifford Pitcher, Guy Bugler.

The Three Horseshoes (now Spyway) Inn, Askerswell, c.1925. The landlady, Sarah Williams, is in the porch, her daughter, Miss E. Williams, on her right.

Askerswell's baker, thought to be called Marsh, poses at the back of the bakery, with his family and the pony that drew his cart, in around 1900. Today the bakehouse is Grey Cottage.

Askerswell Village Fête in the Glebe Field, c.1927. The two girls on the right are Chris Savage and Dorrie Fooks.

Askerswell School dancing team at Blandford Forum in 1959. Among the children are S. Hansford, A. Ascot, D. Knight, S. Ascot, S. Savage, R. Battershall, M. Foot, G. Gillingham, A. Ascot and M. Tricket.

Askserwell Young Farmers Club, 1950. Back row, left to right: Rob Bugler, Bill Hounsell, John Spiller, Dennis Halford, Donald Marsh, Tom Foot, Robert Norton. Middle: George Bryan, Norman Marsh, Gerald Legg, Peggy Pitcher, John Marsh, Muriel Randall, Alan Musgrove, Clifford Pitcher, Jean Biss, Norma Fry, Bill Ives (behind), Elizabeth Buckler. Front: Myriam Bugler, Margery Randall, Mary Foot, Guy Bryan, Kathleen Curran, Janet Spiers, Beryl Osborne.

126

Five

The Char Valley
and Chideock

William Moores jun. (see p. 143) at Stoke Mill, Whitchurch Canonicorum, around 1905. He later sold the pony for £100 in order to get married.

THE NEW COMMERCIAL HOTEL, CHARMOUTH.

The New Commercial Hotel, Charmouth, c.1904. This handsome ivy-clad building later became the (sadly, now closed) New Inn.

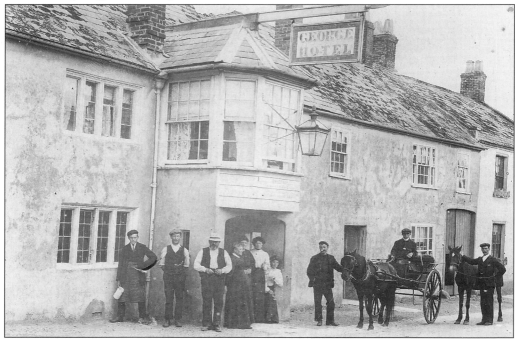

The George Hotel, Charmouth in July 1900, the landlord, Mr J. French and family and staff outside. The handsome lamp above the porch would most likely have been oil lit at the time. The pony and trap was used to convey visitors and was housed in the stables to the right. Left to right: G. Hodges, J. Edwards, J. French, Mrs French, Miss Cook, Miss French, Miss French, J.Bradford, -?-, -?-.

The Post Office, Charmouth, c.1930. This building is now a recently closed shop, the post office having gone off to the lower end of the main street. The postmaster, Mr W.G.B. Holly, published this card.

King Charles House, Charmouth, c.1910. The king spent a night here while trying unsuccessfully to secure a boat for France after the Battle of Worcester. He had arrived from Trent in Somerset with the intention of leaving from Charmouth at midnight on a vessel belonging to Stephen Limbry of nearby Lyme. He waited in vain. Limbry's wife had heard that the king was thought to be in the area (there was a £1,000 reward for him) and locked her husband in his bedroom and, rumour has it, covered any possible escapes by hiding his trousers as well!

Charmouth, c.1907.

Charmouth Fête, 1908. It must have been a hard and dusty march up the hill, especially for the men carrying the banner. Of interest here is the sign 'J. Smith, Fishmonger' on the wall of the thatched house on the left.

The Old Mill and the Bridge, Charmouth, c.1914. The Old Mill in the left background has gone and today's Bridge Street-Wesley Close council estate has taken over. The Dorset Leisure Centre and garage has appeared in the foreground.

Fernhill Corner, Charmouth, c.1932. Almost unrecognisable as today's busy (and controversial) roundabout, where the Lyme Regis-bound traffic leaves the main Charmouth bypass, this was the scene of much excitement in 1929, when a Sangster's lorry carrying a lion ran back down the hill and, after over-hanging branches had ripped the top off the cage, the lion escaped. After it had caused considerable distraction, not least to passing cars, it had to be shot.

This sign was placed on the bridge which took the old coaching road (later A35 trunk road) over the river Char towards Bridport. The county name was erased in 1940 during invasion scares following Dunkirk, but has since been replaced.

The lower end of Charmouth's main street around 1920. Note the shop on the right and the wide open brick drain on the left that was a feature of the village at this time.

High Street (now simply The Street), Charmouth, 1952.

Charmouth Football Club, 1933-34. Highlights of a season which saw the team finish third, a point behind Winsham and Dalwood, in the Perry Street League's Minor (Devon & Dorset) Section, must have been a 10-0 win at home to Lyme Reserves and, later in the season, a 7-3 win at Lyme Regis. A typical line-up that season would have been: E. Dampier, ? Ballard and D. Willard, P. Bowditch, Ron Frampton and W. Smith, H. Boniface, S. Pannel, George Havis, H. Newton and F. Turner. Most of them are in this picture.

VE Day celebrations at Charmouth's Nutcombe Terrace in May 1945. Mrs Pidgeon is on the left; among the children are Angela, Hilary, George and Colin Bowditch, Paulene Turner, Mike Trott and Janet Holman.

Charmouth Football Club, c.1959. Back row, left to right: Charles Stirk (linesman), Doug Stevens, Eddie Austin, Malcolm Bowditch, George Restorick, Brian Bowditch, Tom Norrish. Front: Colin Bowditch, Reg Jones, Bill Draper, Brian Wheller, Fred Helens. In 1960-61 Charmouth set up a new Perry Street League record when they beat Stockland 32-0 at home in a Division Two game. Colin Bowditch scored 14 of the goals, another record which, like the team's total, is still unbeaten in the league today.

The George Hotel, Charmouth, c.1905.

The Street, Charmouth, c.1900. The Royal Oak is the nearest building on the right with the tower of St Andrew's church peeping over the roof.

The Queen's Armes, Charmouth, c.1918. Although far more famous for having housed Charles II soon after the Battle of Worcester (1651), the building gets its Queen's Armes name from its having housed Catherine of Aragon for a night soon after she arrived in England. Today the tea rooms have vanished.

Pebble-picking on Charmouth Beach in 1954. The pebbles, used in industry, were taken to the factory at the edge of the beach where they were collected by lorry. Fears of damage to the foreshore led to the closure of the industry. Here George Bowditch (left) and Grant Edwards are hard at work.

A lorry from Gear's Garage, Charmouth, parked outside the New Inn, Whitchurch Canonicorum while the men enjoy a welcome pint, c.1939. Landlord Arthur Murley is on the right; Mr Quick, a local resident, presumably on his way for his own pint, joins in on the left, and on his left is Sam Farrant. Gear's Garage was in Charmouth's main street; bought by Peter Beecher in the 1960s, it later closed.

Wootton Fitzpaine, c.1920. The Rectory, now a private house, is on the right. The railings on the left have gone and been replaced by houses. To the left rear is the now closed village school with the village hall behind.

Wootton Fitzpaine from the Charmouth Road, c.1920.

Wootton Fitzpaine, c.1920. The tower and bell on the village hall were put there as a memorial to the men of the parish who died during World War One. The open space to the left is now built on.

The cricket pavilion at Charmouth in 1903. The club, once one of the strongest local village sides, was not reformed after World War Two.

The Penn Inn, Charmouth, seen here in the 1920s and burnt down just before World War Two, is said to have been visited by King Charles II during his attempts to escape to France by boat following the Battle of Worcester.

The New Inn, Whitchurch Canonicorum, c.1932, when Arthur Murley (second from left) was the landlord. Originally on the opposite side of the road, this building was erected in 1902 by the Bridport-based Palmers Brewery and closed around 1967 after Murley had been licensee for 40 years.

The Ruby Coach at the The Cross, Whitchurch Canonicorum, 1932. The coach, driven here by Frank Clarke, ran from Charmouth to Bridport.

The Five Bells, Whitchurch Canonicorum, c.1897. The inn, which had the village pound just below, was burnt down on 5 November 1904 and rebuilt. At the time of this picture, the landlord was Samuel George Gifford, who also ran a carriers business to Bridport market; he died twelve months after the inn was burnt down.

The Five Bells, Whitchurch Canonicorum, seen here around 1930, takes its name, like so many other similarly named inns, from the five-bell peal in nearby St Candida's church. The five bells, hung in the tower in the 17th century, were increased to eight earlier this century, but the inn's name remained unchanged.

The bells about to be rehung after tuning at St Wite's (Candida) church, Whitchurch Canonicorum in 1926. Left to right: Mrs Williams, Ern Mills, Ella Slade, Charles Knight, Frank Knight, Gwen Dare, Will Dare, Bert Walborne, Miss Lane.

Whitchurch Canonicorum choir, c.1906. Canon Lee is in the centre and members seen here include Charles Knight and Charles Knight jun.

William Moores and his family at Stoke Mill, Whitchurch Canonicorum, at the turn of the century. Back row, left to right: Rose, William jun., Florrie. Front: Laura, William Moores, Frank, Mrs William Moores, Elsie. Around 1855 a Samuel Moores began a baking and milling business at Stoke Mill baking the bread in the then traditional method with wooden faggots for firing. When the breadmaking was over, Moores added butter and sugar to the left-over dough and, using the dying heat of the ovens, made the now-famous Dorset Knobs (small, round, rusk-like biscuits), said to be so named because they resembled the once traditional Dorset Knob buttons. William Moores followed his father into the business but William jun. continued only as a miller. Samuel Moores's second son, another Samuel, moved in the meantime to Morecombelake and began his own baking business. Although World War Two saw a decline in trade, not least because of man-power problems, a revival, especially of the Dorset Knob biscuits, began in the 1950s, and the business, still in the same family's hands, flourishes today (see pp. 149-50).

Whitchurch Canonicorum bellringers outside the village post office around 1904 include: Henry Jewells, Frank Pitman, William Christopher, Charles Knight sen., Charles Knight jun., Dr Taylor, and Joe Diment.

Whitchurch Canonicorum bellringers in 1904. Left to right: Henry Jewells, Frank Pitman, William Christopher, Charles Knight sen., Charles Knight jun., Dr Taylor, and Joe Diment.

Lower Street, Whitchurch Canonicorum, c.1908.

Whitchurch Canonicorum School with the winners' (?) cup after taking part in the Dorset Choral Association's Scholars Concert on 24 April 1914. A remarkably well-turned-out school for the time.

The first refuse collection in Whitchurch Canonicorum, parked at The Cross in 1932. The board suggests the collection was organised by the Whitchurch & Morecombelake WI.

Charles and Georgina Knight and their family outside Whitchurch Canonicorum post office at the turn of the century. Later the post office moved to a house near Church House, then to the Five Bells, but in 1966 finally returned to the house seen here. The post office has been run by the Knight family for over ninety-five years, and is currently in the charge of 81-year-old Mrs Mary Knight.

Char Valley Horse Show at Whitchurch Canonicorum in a field near the old New Inn in 1939.

Members and juveniles of Whitchurch Canonicorum branch of the National Friendly Society at a club fête day, c.1905. Charles Knight was secretary for thirty-nine years from 1894; his son, Charles jun., joined in 1901 and was still a member in the 1960s.

An old print from the early 19th century of Morecombelake, showing the 'lake' from which the tiny hamlet is said to get its name. Of special interest is the old blacksmiths shop beside the lake; today the Ship Inn is on its immediate left. Behind that is the old post office (left background) then the village shop, the United Reform Chapel, Hill Farm and Lane End.

Sports at Morecombelake Fête, c.1910.

East View Cottage and Moores bakery (left), Morecombelake, c.1898.

Moores Bakery, Morecombelake, c.1950. The thatched cottage seen in the left background in the picture above has gone, and the tall front chimney on the bakery has also disappeared. Note the difference in the road.

S. Moores Bakery, Morecombelake, 1928, with bakers making the famous Dorset Knob biscuits.

Although this card describes this as 'S. Moores Bread Cart at the turn of the century', there is little evidence of any bread being delivered; rather, the cart, which does not bear any name, appears to be carrying (and collecting?) sacks of flour.

St Gabriel's Chapel, Morecombelake, seen here around 1908, was erected in 1841 for 110 sittings with a grant from the Incorporated Society on the condition that 80 of the sittings were free. A tiny nave-only chapel, it was established as a chapel of ease to save locals the long trudge to either Chideock or Charmouth churches.

Manning's Stores, Chideock, c.1906. The shop, hub of the village's life (and gossip), was run for many years (into the 1950s) by Mrs Rose Manning.

Chideock, c.1912. Mr Foss's garage (see below) is on the left (note the Vacuum Oils sign), and the telephone appears to have reached this part of West Dorset.

Foss's Garage, Chideock, c.1941. Kathleen Mary Foss stands beside the shop window and a BP petrol pump. Before eating your heart out at petrol for one shilling and fivepence (7p) a gallon, note the Shell half-gallon dispenser on the right of the garage entrance. Miss Foss later married Wilf Symes, still the popular proprietor of the rebuilt premises.

Chideock, c.1890, looking westwards, with the village shop on the left.

The Broadmead council house estate at Chideock, seen here around 1930, was built around the time of World War One. It had originally been intended to build it in the still-empty field on the opposite (north) side of the main road, but when it was realised that this would mean the front rooms would get the sun throughout the day the houses went up on their present site instead.

Chideock and the entrance to St Giles' church, c.1905. The church, mainly in the Perpendicular style, was restored in 1880. The screen is said to have been taken from a vessel from the Spanish Armada (1588).

Chideock, c.1908. The village school, where Mrs Hurst was a much-loved teacher for over thirty years down to the 1930s, was behind the wall on the left. Closed, and its children now bussed to Bridport, it has made way for two modern houses.

Looking up Duck Street, Chideock, towards St Giles' church, c.1899.

Chideock, c.1901. For many years the post office (immediately past the white, thatched cottage) was run by Charles Gibbs. He carried out the early-morning letter delivery; his daughter Hilda took over for the afternoon post.

Chideock, 1951. White lines have appeared but this part of the A35 Folkstone–Exeter trunk road looks singularly free of the traffic flow that is, at last, to bring the village's long-talked-about bypass.

Seatown around 1905 and shortly after the left-hand extension was added to the Anchor Inn. It is interesting to compare this view with that of over thirty years later on p. 157 and to realise just how little change, apart from the trees that have grown up around Seatown House (on the right) and the toilets on the left, there has been here.

Symondsbury, c.1903.

Seen here on a summer's day in the late 1930s, Seatown is backed by Golden Cap, the highest point (619ft) on the Channel coast. The car park was opened in 1936 as a joint venture by Col. Kitson and Ernest Marsh, who employed Walt Matthew as an attendant. Certainly until 1939, when wartime petrol restrictions (not to mention coastal defences) rendered the car park temporarily redundant, Matthews issued handwritten tickets.

Eype, c.1900. It must have been a tough haul through the narrow lanes for the horse pulling the coal cart.

Charles and Leah Marsh with their thirteen children at Lower Eype Farm, Eype, 1885. Left to right: Laura Lilian, Leah Isobel, Ada Louise, Frederick John, Mabel Laura, Charles Marsh (1837-92), Harriet Ella, Francis Leah, John Alfred, Matthew Charles, Florence Elizabeth, Ernest Richard, Leah Marsh (1838-1915), Ernest Thomas, Sarah Kate.

The New Inn, Eype, c.1938.

In 1929, when John Marsh emigrated to Australia, forty-four years after the picture opposite was taken, the thirteen Marsh children posed together in Bridport. Soon after John's arrival in Australia he was taken ill with appendicitis and operated on by one of the earliest Flying Doctors, on the kitchen table. Standing, left to right: Harriet Ella, Ernest Richard, Sarah Kate, Mabel Laura, Leah Isobel, Ernest Thomas, Laura Lilian. Seated: John Alfred, Francis Leah, Matthew Charles, Frederick John, Ada Louise.

Acknowledgements

We are in debt to Marjorie Mayley for access to material from the collection of her late husband Ken (probably West Dorset's best-known philatelist, and an expert on old pictures of the area), and to Bill Kingman, another philatelist, who was born and bred in Bridport's West Street and, over eighty years later, still lives within sound of the Town Hall bells. Also to the *Bridport News*, especially John Slater and Rosemary Lewis, for permission to use items from their files. The *Bridport News*, of course, has faithfully chronicled Bridport's history since 1855.

Others who have kindly made their own pictures available are Roger Bailey, Donald Balson, Colin Bowditch, Barbara Brook, Jill Bullock, Bill Croad, Colin Derryman, Roger and Deirdre Dowle, M. Evans, John Godfrey, Tony Greenham, Clive and Diana Groves of C.W. Groves & Son, the long-established Bridport Nursery Gardens, Mike Harding of J.C. & R.H. Palmers, Michael Hussey, Mary Jenkins, Geoff Kitton, Alan and Robert Knight, Albert Manley, Brian and Carol Mitchell of the Half Moon Inn, Melplash, Gerald Marsh, Gerald Murley, Cecil Poole, Tim Russ of S.J. Norman & Sons, Philip Saunders, Marjorie Randall, Jim Rowe of R. & C. Snell, the South Street auctioneers, Cyril Tiltman, and Robin Wells.

In a different direction, some research was needed at Bridport Library, where the staff were, as always, more helpful and courteous than duty demands.